The Smile of Thy Love is a lovely window onto 19th-century evangelical piety. Reading it will fuel your desire for holiness and your passion for the lost – all with the bonus of an excellent chapter on visiting the sick.

Tim Chester,
senior faculty member of Crosslands Training and author of
Meeting Christ in the Garden

Today we need more Christians—and especially more pastors—whose love for God's people flows out of their love for God himself. We need men with spiritual roots that deepen as they progress in their service to Christ. Andrew Bonar exemplified this. As God used him more widely, Bonar's private devotion seems to have gone deeper. This brief biographical sketch, pastoral letter, and collection of quotes, introduces readers to a pastor who loved and cared for Christ's church while drawing from a deep spiritual well of God's love in Christ.

Jonathan Master,
President, Greenville Presbyterian Theological Seminary;
author, *Reformed Theology*

The Smile
of Thy Love

The Smile
of Thy Love

A Collection of Quotes from

Andrew
Bonar

CHRISTIAN
HERITAGE
Useful Books of Lasting Value

Copyright © Christian Focus Publications 2024

Hardback ISBN: 978-1-5271-1065-6
Ebook ISBN: 978-1-5271-1119-6

10 9 8 7 6 5 4 3 2 1

First published in 2024
in the Christian Heritage imprint
by
Christian Focus Publications Ltd,
Geanies House, Fearn, Ross-shire,
IV20 1TW, Great Britain

www.christianfocus.com

Cover by Rubner Durais

Typeset by Pete Barnsley (CreativeHoot.com)

Printed by Gutenberg, Malta

CONTENTS

INTRODUCTION

In this short book, we have included a variety of material by Andrew Bonar: (a) a brief biography, (b) a selection of his sayings, (c) a pastoral letter to his congregation in Collace that he wrote from the Holy Land while on a visit to investigate with others the state of the Jews living there, (d) a magazine article he wrote about visiting the sick, and (e) a sermon he preached on the love of the Father.

The congregational letter reveals some of his pastoral concerns. In the magazine article he describes how he engaged in the important ministry of visiting the sick. Concerning the theme of the sermon, he mentions in a letter to his brother Horatius that he had enjoying preaching on it. He wrote: 'I preached lately on "The love of the Father" – one of the sweetest days I ever had in my life. The common truth seemed so fresh and so pleasant to the taste.'

THE LIFE OF
ANDREW BONAR

Andrew Bonar's life covered most of the nineteenth century and he participated in many of the important ecclesiastical changes that occurred in Scotland between 1840 and 1890. Although a quiet man, he became a much-loved and highly admired personality within the Scottish evangelical church. Through his publications and preaching he became connected with a warm style of piety that transcended denominational boundaries. Many of his writings are still in print, which points to the lasting value of what he wrote. His own diary is a wonderful insight into the development of a minister's character throughout the various responsibilities of Christian service – indeed as Bonar's responsibilities become greater, his dedication becomes stronger; yet as his name becomes more eminent, his humility becomes more deep-seated.

Andrew Bonar was one of three brothers, each of whom was a prominent minister in the Free Church of Scotland during the nineteenth-century. The other two were James, a minister in Greenock, and Horatius, a minister in Kelso and then in Edinburgh (he was a hymn-writer and prolific author, with several titles still in print today). The pedigree of Andrew Bonar's family included a long line of ministers, going back to John Bonar (1673–1747), one of the Marrowmen in the early eighteenth-century.

Andrew was born on 29 May 1810, in Edinburgh into a devout family (on the day of his birth, his father recorded that he wished his new son would 'be spared to be a blessing to his friends, and a real member of the Church of Christ' – both desires were fulfilled, although the father did not live to see the fulfilment as he died in 1821, in Andrew's eleventh year). The family attended Lady Glenorchy's Chapel, a staunchly evangelical congregation, although Andrew would not be sure of his conversion to Christ until near the close of 1830.

The family valued education and ensured that Andrew received a good one: at eleven he attended the Edinburgh High School where he was awarded the Dux Gold Medal in 1825; then he went to Edinburgh University, where in 1827 he gained the Gold Medal in the Latin class. It is the case that Andrew had a flair for languages; later on, he was a possible candidate for a Hebrew professorship in one of the Free Church Colleges (his commentaries on Leviticus and on the Psalms reveal his competency in this regard).

Andrew chose to enter the Divinity Hall of Edinburgh University where one of the professors was Thomas Chalmers. After an inner struggle, he determined that he wanted to be sure of his conversion before he would begin such study. He could have entered the Divinity Hall in 1829, but it took over a year before he had assurance of his salvation. His diary suggest that he had been converted earlier than 1830, but for various reasons he had failed to see that he had faith in Christ. He mentions that he rested much upon his prayers and desires to be holy instead of relying on Jesus. There was a legalistic aspect to his outlook and a failure to focus on the love of Jesus. He also sensed that he was at times seeking for approval from men rather than God. He admitted to his brother John that his mind wandered during sermons and he was not really affected by the threatenings of God against sinners. While he did not realise it then, he was being prepared for pastoral interactions with others who would go through similar meanderings in their search for assurance, and he was able from his own experience to direct them away from focussing on themselves and to concentrate on Jesus instead.

A book that brought real benefit to him at that time of seeking assurance was William Guthrie's *The Christian's Great Interest*. On Sunday, 17 October

1830, he records (On the margin for this date is written, 'assurance begun'): 'In reading Guthrie's *Saving Interest* I have been led to hope that I may be in Christ though I have never yet known it. All the marks of faith in a man which he gives are to be found in me, I think, although very feeble. This is the first beam of joy, perhaps, that I have yet found in regard to my state, and yet it is scarcely more than a hope.' Two weeks later he records, 'For about two weeks past, ever since I read a passage in Guthrie's *Saving Interest*, I have had a secret joyful hope that I really have believed on the Lord Jesus.'

After coming to assurance of salvation, Andrew does not seem to have ever lost it. In 1892, he confessed, 'It was in the year 1830 that I found the Saviour, or rather, that He found me and laid me on His shoulders rejoicing, and I have never parted company with Him all these sixty-two years.'

PREPARATION FOR MINISTRY

When he completed his studies in the Divinity Hall, Andrew began practical preparation for the ministry. As he anticipated future service, he recorded his longing in his Diary on 26 June 1835: 'Oh may He be with me where I go, and send a revival in the parish where I am now to preach and work, showing the truth of a Saviour crucified to the heart of every one.' That prayerful desire was to be amply fulfilled.

Bonar first went to serve as a summer missionary in Jedburgh in the south of Scotland with Rev. John Purves (his wife was Andrew's cousin). So he was licensed there to preach by the Presbytery on July 1, and preached his first sermon on the following Sunday. A prominent feature of his time in Jedburgh was visiting prisoners and speaking to them about their souls. He also engaged in evangelistic activities among old and young. During his time there, he continued to read works of theology and mentions Thomas Goodwin's book *Christ Set Forth* as well as the *Marrow of Modern Divinity*.

The following year found him in Edinburgh as the assistant to Robert S. Candlish in St George's. Candlish was one of the leaders of the Evangelical party in the Church of Scotland and eventually became very prominent in the Free Church after 1843. He was also a great preacher, able to sway large crowds by his eloquent manner in preaching the gospel. Bonar had some difficulty in moving there due to the wishes of Mr Purves for him to stay in Jedburgh and continue in the work that had begun to flourish. Yet Andrew was certain that it was God's call to go: he found guidance from relevant Scriptures (the situation in Acts 20 when Paul left a situation that seemed prosperous), prayer, conversation with others, and from Christian literature (he was helped by two chapters in Krummacher's *Elijah the Tishbite*).

Bonar's time as Candlish's assistant was a period of inner reflection as to his calling. Initially he was not required to preach and he found this aspect difficult to cope with, especially as his brother Horatius and his friends Robert M'Cheyne and Alexander Somerville seemed to be in more suitable locations as far as preaching was concerned. Instead his role was that of visiting homes in areas round the church. Jedburgh had been a more rural area, whereas St George's was in the heart of Edinburgh. In a sense, these places are similar to where he would minister later – the rural parish of Collace in Perthshire and the urban community of Finnieston in Glasgow.

Bonar wondered why God was bringing him along this road at St George's and early on deduced that the Lord was teaching him important lessons. One was the cause of his sense of discontent and he concluded that his 'present unhappiness rose from my unwillingness to be humbled and be nothing' (Sunday, 8 January 1837). Another lesson, recorded that same day, concerned the centrality of Jesus and Bonar records his thoughts on this matter in some beautiful words: 'I desire now just to enjoy Christ as my Lord and my Friend, and let Him send me among men, or keep me unknown and unoccupied, as He pleases.'

Eventually doors opened for preaching, both in connection to his role as Candlish's assistant and also elsewhere. A year later he recorded, 'In looking back,

I regard nothing of my sore perplexity and trouble; they have taught me much and led me near to God. Now my work in Rose Street is prospering much. A hundred and twenty attentive souls on Sunday evening at the meeting, and some cases wherein the Lord appears to be blessing my labour' (Wednesday 20 December 1837). He also records a very important practical conviction that he had learned by experience: 'More and more convinced, by the very want of it, that the way to be successful is to be within the sanctuary with God, and then come out to the people' (Saturday, 23 December 1837).

Another development that occurred during his time as Candlish's assistant was interest in Jewish mission by several people within his denomination and personal increase of contact with Jews. This was to lead to him being asked later to go to Palestine on a fact-finding journey to discover the state of Jews living there.

MINISTRY IN COLLACE, PERTHSHIRE

Bonar finally commenced his first pastorate on 20 September 1838, when he was inducted to the parish of Collace in Perthshire. Obviously that day was very important to him and it is interesting to observe what was on his mind. His diary informs us that he was conscious of his sinful tendencies and that 'the minister should wash in the blood of Christ before going to proclaim with voice of thanksgiving God's salvation for men'. He 'wished for deeper views of my sinfulness in its length and breadth, that I might feel as Paul, and go to present myself just as an empty vessel which the Lord is to fill.' And he wanted to 'receive the spirit of love, affection for the people, and anxiety about the old minister's soul, and may I receive this at ordination.' In particular Isaiah 11:1-9 was on his heart, so that he would 'be like Christ, daily His witness, His Spirit of wisdom and understanding teaching me the Scriptures.' Imagine his joy when the presiding minister specifically mentioned this passage as he laid hands on Bonar. It is not surprising that Bonar's response was that 'in great calmness and strong desire I gave myself to God my Saviour, and expected henceforth His promised Spirit.' Surely such an ordination was a sign of good things to come. The reason he was so concerned was that there was probably only half a dozen real Christians in the parish, and the aged parish minister who was still there when Bonar was inducted was not one of them.

Collace was a fairly remote parish and was not an evangelical one when he went there. Its previous minister had no interest in evangelical matters, even voting against them in the Presbytery after Bonar had been inducted. Yet the wind of God was blowing there as well as in other places throughout Scotland at that time, and the congregation in Collace quickly became evangelical in tone, and Bonar saw some regular growth, especially in the early years of his ministry. His ministry commenced as developments concerning patronage in the Church of Scotland were coming to a crisis, and which resulted in the formation of the Free Church of Scotland in 1843.

Bonar was to minister in Collace from 1838 to 1856, almost two decades of spiritual service to his Master. During those years, he had several privileges given to him. In the spring and summer of 1839, he went as one of the group of four sent to investigate the state of the Jews in Palestine and Eastern Europe. He also became well-known as an author with several volumes published. They included an account of the journey to assess the Jewish world called *Narrative of a Mission to the Jews* (1842), *Memoir of Rev. R. M. McCheyne* (1843), a commentary on Leviticus (1845), a volume on Christ's second coming called *Redemption Draweth Nigh* (1847), a small book on *The Gospel Pointing to the Person of Christ* (1852), *Nettleton and His Labours* (1854), and *The Visitor's Book of Texts* (1855).

His best-known work, *The Memoirs of McCheyne*, was put together in a very short period of time, in about four months from September to December 1843, and in an unusual method of launching a book he arranged for a day of prayer and fasting. The effect of McCheyne's life and death never left Bonar. That was the low personal point of those years in Collace whereas the high point was his marriage to Isabella Dickson and their subsequent children. During those years, he had several calls to other congregations, including as a missionary to the Jews, but he did not sense God was causing him to move from Collace until he was asked to move to Glasgow in 1858.

MINISTRY IN FINNIESTON, GLASGOW

Finnieston was a new venture by a Glasgow Free Church congregation called St Matthew's, similar to what we would call a church plant today. In 1856 they founded Finnieston Free Church, with the building being opened in the December of that year. The initial building was used until 1878 when a new one was erected. Bonar was minister there from 1858 to 1892. In 1858, the attendance numbered about 250, but it eventually grew to over 1,000.

During his years in Glasgow Bonar continued to write or edit books. His own work on the psalms was published in 1859 with the title, *Christ and His Church in the Book of Psalms*; the *Memoir of David Sandeman* (a missionary in China) appeared in 1860; he also wrote *Memorials of Rev. J. Allen*, an assistant minister in Bonar's congregation who died at a young age; he edited his edition of the *Scots Worthies* (1879) and his editions of the *Letters of Samuel Rutherford* (1862, 1891); he wrote a book for young people called *Palestine for the Young* (1865); the *Brook Besor* was written for burdened Christians (1879); and the *Life of Rev. James Scott* (1885).

Above the door of his new church, Bonar caused to be engraved in Hebrew the words, 'He that winneth souls is wise.' This was an attempt, among others, to reach Jews living in Glasgow. In fulfilment of this verse, Bonar engaged in regular evangelism himself, including open-air preaching and visitation. He soon became a well-known figure in the area, and his friendly way of speaking and behaving made him acceptable to all ages, including children. One child called him 'the minister with the laughing face', a description that speaks volumes. The congregation became a spiritual home for believers in the surrounding community. In addition, Bonar encouraged all kinds of evangelistic events, be they those associated with Moody and Sankey or children's meetings led by an evangelist called Hammond.

Sadly, his wife passed away in 1864 from complications related to childbirth, and we can read of his deep sorrow in his Diary. Ten years later, in 1874, he received the degree of DD from Edinburgh University, and in 1878 he was Moderator of the Free Church General Assembly (a difficult year because of the concern about matters of Higher Criticism connected to an Old Testament higher critical scholar called William Robertson Smith). In 1881 he visited America, spoke at the Northfield Conference connected to D. L. Moody, and visited sites connected to one of his heroes, Jonathan Edwards. Bonar reached his Jubilee in the ministry in 1888 and his congregation showed their appreciation of his ministry by giving him the astonishing gift of £4,000. Three years later, in 1891, when he was over eighty, he asked for an assistant and David M. McIntyre was called as his colleague and eventual successor. He later married Bonar's third daughter, Jane Christian Bonar. Subsequently he became Principal of the Bible Training Institute in Glasgow.

In December 1892, Andrew Bonar died very peacefully, and went to his reward. He experienced the day he had often wrote about when he would be united with family and friends who had gone before him, but more importantly found himself in the presence of the Saviour he had served so wholeheartedly and well.

SAYINGS

ASSURANCE

'Assurance is not a privilege only, but a duty.'

'The youngest believer is entitled to full assurance.'

'Learn to read your title to the family of God by what
God has said, not by a special
message to yourself.'

'There are three kinds of assurance mentioned in
the Word, and they are often misunderstood. The
first is assurance of faith (Heb. 10:22), certainty of
acceptance, arising from the belief of God's testimony.
2. Full assurance of understanding (Col. 2:2), the soul
getting more and more established according as it sees
the fulness and riches of Christ. 3. Assurance of hope
(Heb. 6:11), which is the saved man, in possession
of acceptance, looking into the future for the things
hoped for, sure he shall yet have them all.'

BACKSLIDING

'If at any time we lose the sense of his presence, the
way to get it back is not by sitting down to "count our
evidences". It is by coming back to him.'

'Christ utilises even the backslidings of his people for their further good.'

'If you can do without the blood you are a backslider.'

'Knowledge of Christ is the preventive of backsliding. It fills the heart, and that keeps the world out.'

'Peter traces backsliding to forgetfulness. Let us ask the Lord to give us better memories for all his benefits.'

CHRISTIAN SERVICE

'God fills our hands with work, but he does not overburden us. When we are overburdened it is time for us to stop.'

'Have glanced now and then at what God may have sent me to do, but as yet no opening. There are two great lessons to me at present: willing to be nothing, if God so please, and prayer for the past opportunities being blessed. I feel as if God had put me now for a time in a lower place of his vineyard, [with] less work.'

'Some good men are very peremptory in asking God to give them souls. That may not be the best service you can do for God. The best service you can give him is to submit to his will!'

'The way to rise high in Christ's kingdom is to serve much.'

'Self-forgetting work is heavenly work.'

'The best part of Christian work is that part which only God sees.'

'There may be real submission to the will of God while we can't help wishing things were otherwise. God does not ask us to feel that everything is for the best, but he does ask us to believe it.'

'It is natural for us to think if we could do some great exploit, or carry through some great piece of self-denial, we should be high in the kingdom. But it is not so. It is doing something that nobody sees but the Master himself, and no one knows but he.'

'Service for the Master that everybody praises is very dangerous service. Perhaps in the day the Master returns the name of one we never heard of in the

Church of Christ may be the highest, because he did most, simply for the Master.'

'Christ meets us in the path of duty. If the women had stayed at the sepulchre they would have missed the meeting with Christ.'

'God may have given you some work to do for him in the position in which he has placed you which no one else could do if you were to leave it undone. We should be very careful how we wish to change from whatever position in life into which God has seen fit to put us.'

FAITH

'Faith does a great deal for us. It unites us to Christ. Hope does a great deal for us. How it brightens the future! But love flows out of ourselves to others.'

'If any of you ask, what is great faith? The reply is, having a great opinion of Christ.'

'Great faith is simple faith. If you are seeking great faith, remember, the simpler it is, the greater it will be.'

'There was a defect in the faith of many who came to Christ to be healed. But it was not the strength

of their faith Christ looked to, but the reality
of it. They got the cure though the hand that
touched him trembled.'

'When we weep over Christ's sufferings merely
because they are sad and sorrowful, that is feeling.
When we weep because of the sin that made him
suffer, and see that he suffered for us, that is faith.'

'Who is it who obtains the victory over the world? Is
it he who is in the midst of favourable circumstances,
with nothing to draw him from the right path? No;
the victorious man is the man of faith – a faith in
God that will overcome difficulties.'

FELLOWSHIP

'I see plainly that fellowship with God is not means
to an end, but is to be the end itself. I am not to use it
as a preparation for study or for Sabbath labour, but
as my chiefest end, the likest thing to heaven.'

'Fellowship with God is very much the same
thing as assurance.'

'It is in the secret of his presence that we get our souls
replenished with the Holy Ghost.'

'The nearer you come to him the better, for you will then be further from the world, and the world will have least power over you.'

'When men seek to entice you to forego communion with God and to follow the world with them, let your face shine with the brightness that comes from your communion with the Master, and they will cease to trouble you. Christians can sometimes do more by shining for God than by speaking for him.'

'I want to live in the love of God, for God, enjoying God, glorifying God, and every day able to tell what new discovery I have made in the fulness of Christ.'

'Our one great hindrance to fuller blessing is something along with God in our heart.'

GOD

'What is a perfection in God should be a quality in us.'

'Thus we see that this Psalm (139) is one of joy and happy confidence in God, abounding in views that enlarge the heart and strengthen it. It expresses the worshipper's happy remembrance of the omniscient and omnipresent God.'

'Judge of God's love only by his unspeakable gift – a gift irrevocably given and given to you – never by frames and states and feelings and your own thoughts.'

'God is able to love us without a cause though we hated him without a cause.'

'He giveth grace to the humble, to those who do not come with a price in their hand, who simply expect it as a gift. "He giveth grace to the lowly," who bring their empty vessels and say, "Lord, fill them!"'

'God can do more on earth than in heaven for the glory of his name.'

'A God not seen through Christ is no God at all.'

GRATITUDE

'Let me record it to the praise of the glory of Divine grace and infinite mercy, that for many years, indeed as many as I can remember, since my first discovery of the sinner's way to God by Christ, I have never been allowed to lose my way to the mercy seat for a single day. I have not always had bright sunshine, but I have every day had sunlight and not darkness in my soul. What shall I render to the Lord?'

HEAVEN

'Well may I glory in being a citizen of Zion, for many shall be proud of their relation to it when the cities of the nations have long been forgotten.'

'I often exult in the thought that every moment in the ages to come I shall be better and better able to love him who loved me from all eternity – who chose me – who lived for me that life of obedience, and died that death in order that I, a soul that sinned, might live with him for ever.'

'There is joy even in happy heaven when a sinner is saved, so that every Sabbath heaven is getting happier, because lost souls are being found.'

'If you ask me, what is glory? Well, I can't tell you, but I know that it is a hundred times better than grace.'

'It is to show the "exceeding riches of his grace" that the Lord gives a whole eternity of blessedness to the man who, like the dying thief, has only been leaning on him for a few hours.'

'Are you not "looking for and hasting unto the coming of the day of God"? You and I shall then stand in our Redeemer's beauty, all fair, no spot, without blemish, without wrinkle, white and clean, in fine linen, in garments of needlework, like Jesus. Will you know me in that day? Will you know yourself?'

'They go on for ever from strength to strength, revelling in discoveries of the name of God, led by the Lamb for ever in the green pastures, and to living fountains of water. Who can imagine how deep will be their holiness, as thus they grow up to the fulness of the stature of Christ – into him who is the Head?'

'Suppose that I, a sinner, be walking along yon golden street, passing by one angel after another. I can hear them say as I pass through their ranks, "A sinner! A crimson sinner!" Should my feet totter? Should my eye grow dim? No: I can say to them, "Yes, a sinner, a crimson sinner, but a sinner brought near by a forsaken Saviour, and now a sinner who has boldness to enter into the Holiest through the blood of Jesus."'

'We are to be rewarded, not only for work done, but for burdens borne, and I am not sure but that the brightest rewards will be for those who have borne burdens without murmuring. On that day he will take the lily, that has been growing so long among thorns, and lift it up to be the glory and wonder of all the universe; and the fragrance of that lily will draw forth ineffable praises from all the hosts of heaven.'

'Oh what will it be to hear Christ singing then, leading the song of praise, and inviting all the ransomed to join him! Our voices are only now being tuned for that day when we shall join him in "the song of the Lamb" – a song which shall be for ever, and ever, and ever.'

HOLINESS AND CHRISTIAN LIVING

'Remember the Master's standard of holiness is, "They are not of the world, even as I am not of the world" (John 17:14, 16).'

'A great feature of holiness is power to bear hard and heavy burdens.'

'A believer is not very holy if he is not very kind.'

'No one will ever be holy who is not much
alone with God.'

'I think it is a very poor kind of holiness that does not
make us care for others.'

'Many souls are being exercised about holiness, but
not equally about righteousness. Holiness is the
hidden thing we cannot see; righteousness is the
manifestation of holiness in act and life.'

'A holy life is made up of a number of small things;
little words, not eloquent speeches or sermons;
little deeds, not miracles of battle nor one great
heroic act of mighty martyrdom, make up the true
Christian life.'

'The avoidance of little evils, little sins, little
inconsistencies, little weaknesses, little follies,
indiscretions, and imprudences, little foibles, little
indulgences of the flesh; the avoidance of such little
things as these goes far to make up at least the
negative beauty of a holy life.'

'The man who believes on the Lord Jesus keeps all
the ten commandments.'

'A gloomy believer is surely an anomaly in Christ's kingdom.'

'Perhaps you would have grown in grace far more if you had used what God has given you for him, and forgotten about yourself.'

'There are some saints who weep so much over their imperfect holiness that they never rejoice.'

'A saint without the help of the Holy Spirit can no more walk in the light as God is in the light than a sinner can be justified apart from the shedding of the blood without which there is no remission.'

'It is as impossible to alter God's law as to alter his throne. You cannot get above the law. Then get deeper and deeper in sympathy with it, because that law is the mind of God.'

'If you do not indulge in godly sorrow, is it not likely you are losing a good deal of sanctification? Have we nothing to repent of? No wasted hours? How little we have done for God! Ah, that we had prayed more!'

'It is a grace to give reproof rightly, and it is a grace to take it rightly. You may be sure you are safe in giving reproof if it costs you pain to do it. Rightly given reproof is sometimes a means of conversion.'

'I sometimes feel as if there were two sides to my soul, the one looking earthward, the other heavenward.'

'Follow the Shepherd, and remember if you are following him you will be sure to get a mouthful of pasture every now and then. Our Shepherd would not lead us where nothing is to be found.'

'We are fed on the same food as those who have gone before us. They are on one side of the mountain in the sunshine, and we are on the other side in the shadow, but we are both getting the same pasture.'

'It is what we have seen and known of Christ that gives us communion, not what we have discovered of our own infirmities.'

'I have been getting remarkable glimpses of Divine love in answer to earnest prayer that I might know "the love that passeth knowledge".'

'We have but one thing to do, we have but one Person to please. Has your life been thus simplified?'

'We have more to do with the world to come than with this world.'

'The world is all that is outside of the soul's spiritual life.'

'I am more than ever convinced that unholiness lies at the root of our little success. "Holy men of God" spake to the fathers. It must be holy men still that speak with power.'

'It is a rule in the Christian life that one grace exercised strengthens the other graces.'

'We don't live upon experiences, but we ought to grow in experiences.'

'The joy of holiness is often sweeter than the joy of forgiveness, for the joy of holiness implies fellowship with God.'

'I discover that very small distractions may become very great temptations.'

'Ask any gardener, and he will tell you it is a sad indication of any plant to stop growing.'

'If you would really win the crown you must keep fast hold of the Cross.'

'The safe side is Christ's side. He gets no wound in all his battles. He is conqueror in all he undertakes.'

'We are called "more than conquerors" not at the end of our course, but while it is going on.'

'You need not be afraid of too much grace. Great grace never makes a man proud. A little grace is very apt to make a man be puffed up.'

'The man who sees Christ in life is sure to see him in the valley of the shadow of death.'

'A man is never safe in rebuking another if it does not cost him something to have to do it.'

'If the Father has the kingdom ready for us, he will take care of us on the way.'

'We do not need new swords, new spears, new arms. We only need more eye-salve to see who is on our side.'

'Lot would not give up Christ, but he would not give up much for Christ.'

'Give us a taste of the grapes of Eshcol that we may long for the Promised Land.'

'Let us be as watchful after the victory as before the battle.'

'O make us sincere to the core of our heart by the help of thy Holy Spirit, for it is not natural!'

'Vessels are not fountains. Vessels need to be filled as well as to give out to others.'

HUMILITY

'It is not the sight of our sinful heart that humbles us; it is a sight of Jesus Christ. I am undone because mine eyes have seen the King.'

'Enable me to live under the smile of thy love, willing not to be noticed upon earth, if so I may glorify thee more.'

'The Lord has been teaching me to be willing to be least of all and servant of all. The soul of a weaned child is what I seek: meek and lowly in heart, with the eye upon the Lord alone. In this there is rest to the soul.'

'It takes us all our days to learn these two things – to be meek and to be lowly.'

'It is a test of our progress in sanctification if we are willing to have our faults pointed out to us, without getting angry. Why should we take offence at being told we are not perfect?'

'God tells us to love reproof. I don't know any man who ever took reproof better than Eli. "It is the Lord." When Nathan said to David, "Thou art the man," he did not flare up as Herod did. No; he said, "I have sinned," and went away to write the fifty-first Psalm.'

'There are some people who can stand anything but flattery. If no one ever praises you, you are all the better for it.'

JESUS

'Do not try to put religion in the place of Christ. The heart of religion is to know Christ, and to know him better, and to know him still better. Then to see him as he is, and then to be like him.'

'Draughts of the water of life are just fresh views of Christ.'

'Each plant needs a whole sun, and each of us needs a whole Saviour.'

'Those who have real love to Christ always wish they had more.'

'The promises are streams coming down from the heart of Christ.'

'The person of the God-man presents thoughts, and declares truths, and reveals feelings towards us, such as may well cause a soul to cry, "All my springs are in thee."'

'The Shepherd can number his sheep, but the sheep can't. Christ's favourite expression, when speaking of his saved ones, is "many".'

JESUS, HIS LIFE

'He is our peace, not by his death only, but by his life of obedience also, imputed to us.'

'His *dying* was fully sufficient to remove the guilt of my conception, and my connection with Adam; while his *doing* was holy from the womb.'

'His life above is a life of love, no less than was his life below.'

'Christ's obedience was his taking up our undone work.'

'His life of obedience – you know what it was. A walk from Bethlehem to Calvary without a stumble.'

'Christ came to provide us with righteousness undefiled, he obeyed for us perfectly. In that robe he walked through our world every day, and when he had finished his walk, as Elijah left his mantle to Elisha, the Saviour left his robe for us to wear.'

'Christ's body and soul, all his person and all his acts were holy. His walk was holy, and his inmost affections holy.'

JESUS, HIS CROSS

'There is room at the cross for any sinner, and the Gospel invites me, as a sinner among the rest, to hear what the cross says.'

'It is wonderful that now for fifty years the Lord has kept me within sight of the Cross.'

'The drawing love of the cross of Christ (looking for a moment at the matter from man's point of view) surely appeals as readily and suitably to the hearts of children as to adults.'

'God's people have a ravenous hunger for a crucified Christ.'

JESUS, IN GLORY

'Let us often stay to rejoice that the Man of Sorrows is happy now – "most blessed for ever!"'

'O how his beauty shall burst forth when the King appears with his many crowns!'

'No Christian denies the fact of the Second Coming of Christ. But very many, even of the most godly in later days, have failed to meditate much upon this blessed hope.'

'All the glories of his kingdom will be only so many channels for conveying manifestations of himself to his redeemed. Godhead for evermore discovered to us by means of God in our nature, this is the chiefest joy.'

'I find the thought of Christ's coming very helpful in keeping me awake. Those who are waiting for his appearing will get a special blessing. Perhaps they will get nearer to his Person. I sometimes hope it will be so, and that he will beckon me nearer to him if I am waiting for him.'

MEDITATION

'There are things God will show you in meditation that you will not find in the preaching of the Word, or in the assembly of believers.'

'Meditation is letting God speak to us till our heart is throbbing.'

'Have been able, amid much business, to get much of this day for prayer and meditation, having got preparation forward yesterday in great measure. Such a time is like climbing up the mount, and looking all around in calmness, seeing what our inheritance is, and thus better able to ask many things. O what a sense of poverty comes over me, looking at that wealth!'

'When you have got a blessing, take time to let it sink into your own heart before you tell it out.'

'Look into the fountain, and the very looking will make you thirsty.'

'More carefully than ever I hope this year to give two hours before going out every day to meditation on the Word and prayer.'

'Think upon the Lord while you can, and he will think upon you when you can't.'

'You will soon be a king. Why not think of your kingdom?'

'Union to Christ's person is a fact in the case of every believer, and ought therefore to be a constant subject of meditation to every believer.'

'When we dwell on the Saviour's Person we are in his company. Faith places us by his side, and shows us his glory, until what we see makes our heart burn within us.'

'Preach Christ, for you cannot preach Christ without preaching sin.'

'The Cross was the breaking of God's alabaster box, the fragrance of which has filled heaven and earth.'

'The Gospel is like the sun – it can look in
at any window.'

'Many things have made earth to me more than ever
a wilderness and a land of broken cisterns, but the
Lord Jesus is more than ever a full heaven to me.'

MINISTERS

'Ministers are specially under God's eye; he
sees if they walk in the steps of Jesus in their
chambers and at their studies. They must be ever
separated to the Lord.'

'Ministers of Christ may be guilty of leading others
into sin, if they do aught to create levity in the
people's minds, or aught that may lessen the holy
feeling of reverence toward God.'

'The sins of teachers are the teachers of sins. Beware
of the bad things of good men.'

'Felt in sorrow this morning in reviewing my ministry.
So little fruit, and of late so much preaching and no
fruit at all to my knowledge. This is the day in the
Assembly when all the ministers and elders are to be
humiliating themselves for these things before God.

Lord, Lord, break my hard heart. Lord, show why thou hidest thy face from me. Wilt thou not from this day make me wise to win souls.'

'Have seen more than ever yet my real backsliding. I am a backslider both as a man and as a minister. Close walking with God; daily, if not hourly, taste of the sweetness of Christ; self-denial in setting aside temptation; all these must now be sought by me. O God of grace, return to me from this day! O to win Christ! O to be as Enoch till I die!'

'I think I have got more good from visiting my people than from any book of practical theology I ever read.'

PERSONAL DISSATISFACTION

'I lament the sins of coldness and earthliness; wandering in prayer; seeking to benefit others without being benefited myself; something of discontent at little annoyances; chagrin and envy; opportunities lost; sick persons ill-advised; my class of young people too little taught Christ; and in all my preaching very inadequate setting forth of Christ and the Spirit.'

'I feel my unholiness, my prayerlessness, and my
want of solemnity and sense of responsibility. I seem
to have done nothing at all for this people, and
I wonder much at my indifference to the salvation of
the old minister; and my little regret at the expressed
indifference of neighbouring clergymen. I feel also
a great deal of envy at hearing of others' success.'

PRAISE

'We should be always wearing the garment of praise,
not just waving a palm now and then!'

'Many a temptation has been baffled, many
a difficulty faced successfully, and many a sorrow
calmed by a song of praise.'

PRAYER

'Let us seek to be delivered from trifling prayers, and
contentment with trifling answers.'

'I was living very grossly, namely, labouring night
and day in visiting, with very little prayerfulness.
I did not see that prayer should be the main
business of every day.'

'Prayer will be very lame and dry if it does not come from reading the Scriptures.'

'O brother, pray; in spite of Satan, pray; spend hours in prayer; rather neglect friends than not pray; rather fast, and lose breakfast, dinner, tea, and supper – and sleep too – than not pray. And we must not talk about prayer, we must pray in right earnest.'

'Is not this a lamentable state of things that there should be so much to get and so few to ask!'

'Fasting is abstaining from all that interferes with prayer.'

'I spent till midday fasting and praying. I sought as much to be drawn into his presence and to himself as weaned from the world.'

'It is a sign that the blessing is not at hand when God's people are not praying much.'

'Ask God for anything, but let him judge as to the manner and measure of the giving.'

'The reason so many of the prayers of God's people bring down no answer is, they do not come from communion.'

'When you begin to pray, always get into this position, leaning on his bosom. Don't pray to some one far off. Don't pray even to some one in the same room.'

'The blessing we pray for may not come at once, but it is on its way. Sometimes the Lord keeps us waiting long because he likes to keep us in his presence.'

'It is my deepest regret that I pray so little. I should count the days, not by what I have of new instances of usefulness, but by the times I have been enabled to pray in faith and to take hold upon God.'

'Oh, believing friends, ask for all ministers and teachers of the Word this power and presence of the Holy Ghost. We would not need so much speaking if we had this presence and power.'

'If we had prayed more, we need not have worked so hard. We have too little praying face to face with God every day. Looking back at the end I suspect there will be great grief for our sins of omission – omission to get from God what we might have got by praying.'

'Persevering prayerfulness – day by day wrestling and pleading – is harder for the flesh than preaching.'

'When we pray in the morning to be filled with
the Spirit, may we expect to be filled all day with
thoughts of Christ.'

'In prayer in the wood for some time, having set apart
three hours for devotion; felt drawn out much to pray
for that peculiar fragrance which believers have about
them, who are very much in fellowship with God. It is
like an aroma, unseen but felt. Other Christians have
the beauty of the Rose of Sharon.'

'Hezekiah's prayer got a large answer. When you send
in a petition to the Lord, leave a wide margin, that he
may write a great deal on it.'

'When you find a promise it will not fall into your
lap. You must shake the tree by prayer.'

'It is not right for God's people to say when a matter
for prayer is put before them, "Oh, what can my
prayers do?" What can your God do?'

'Lord, use me yet! Lord, I love thee and thy work; give
me souls still before my sun has set, and give me more
grace and knowledge of Christ. My light in daily life
is very dim, I fear. But I shall see Christ glorified by
the multitudes he has saved by others, and I shall
rejoice in his joy.'

PREACHING

'I wish to pray from this date every Sabbath morning before going out to preach, and every time I go to preach to stand still a little and praise the Lord for sending to sinners his glorious gospel.'

'I now try to pray every Sabbath before leaving the pulpit: "Lord, give fruit, forgive the sin; fill me with the Spirit again and again, and accept my praise."'

'I preached lately on the love of the Father – one of the sweetest days I ever had in my life! The common truth seemed so fresh and so pleasant to the taste.'

'Christ is more than ever precious to me in his atonement, righteousness, merit, heart. Nothing else satisfies me. I only yearn to know him better, and preach him more fully.'

'There are two things which we must uphold and hold fast – the sacrifice of Christ upon the cross, and the priesthood of Christ in heaven.'

'Have been taught that joy in the Spirit is the frame in which God blesses us to others. Joy arises from fellowship with him – I find that whatever sorrow or humiliation of spirit presses on us, that should give way in some measure to a fresh taste of God's love when going forth to preach.'

'Did you ever feel in preaching as if you were a blunt arrow? I felt so yesterday until about evening, when the Archer seemed to sharpen the point.'

'Use for yourself first what the Lord teaches you, and if he spare you, use it for others.'

'Continued omission of the Gospel in our sermons, or passing from it quickly, arises from self-righteousness. We feel as if there was not so much need of pressing this truth. Whereas self-righteousness in minister and people is such that nothing but incessant repetition of the gospel can be right.'

SACRAMENTS

'The sacraments of the New Testament are signs between heaven and earth. Baptism is a sign from heaven that God remembers little children, and looks upon them in love, saying, "Suffer little children to come unto me" etc. The Lord's Supper is a sign from earth to heaven that we remember our Lord's dying command: "This do in remembrance of me"; and keep it till he come.'

'I consider the baptism of infants to be, not a confession of our faith, but of God's interest in us. I am in the way of putting it thus: "Remember, parents, to tell your children that on the day of baptism they were presented to the Three Persons, and the water was meant to be a sign and seal that Father, Son, and Holy Spirit offered salvation to them. Ask them, 'Have you accepted the gift offered?'"'

'When we come to the communion table today let us remember at what a tremendous cost our redemption was purchased; our fellowship secured; our communion with God restored. And as you remember this, see that you enter fully into, and enjoy without fear the fellowship he has thus secured to us.'

'If Christ were visiting personally our communion table, to how many he might say, "O fools! slow to believe all that the prophets have spoken!" Why is the Bible so little known, read, studied, prayed over, fed upon? Why, believer, are you not more conversant with the thoughts of God, given forth to us from Genesis to Revelation?'

'Let us go, then, to the Table rejoicing that we have this full access, and pleading these three hours of the Surety's darkness as the very reason for our enjoying light and sunshine.'

'As the bread is broken and the wine is poured out, may we feel that he is scarcely an absent Saviour, though unseen.'

'A most blessed day. At the table, when giving thanks, I felt as if I could have stood there for ever to praise the Lord for his grace. I realised the blessedness of eternal praise in heaven.'

'This Communion morning got some view of how deep may be the holy peace of a soul that sees the vastness of the Saviour's grace.'

'I rode up to Blairgowrie to the Lord's Supper, I felt that there the Gift of God to sinners and the heart of God to sinners are so fully and exclusively set forth that the Lord's table is really the stereotyping of the gospel.'

'However weak you are, if you value supremely the atoning blood, come to the table.'

'At the Communion table remember him and forget yourself.'

'There is nothing between a sinner and the Saviour, but there is something between the sinner and the Lord's table.'

'Jesus is walking to-day among the seven golden candlesticks, and he will stop here at our Communion table, to see if any of us want anything from him.'

THE HOLY SPIRIT

'The man who reads the Old and New Testament without assuming the Spirit as the inspirer of all, will never find the hid treasures there.'

'Every line in this inspired Bible is wet with the dew of the Spirit's love.'

'The kind, patient, longsuffering love of the Spirit is infinitely wonderful.'

'The Spirit of liberty delivers us from the bondage of mere religion. He not only does this in a certain measure, but in a very full measure. He brings us into a large place. You are not to think he takes us out of the deep waters and makes us stand shivering on the shore.'

'I long more and more to be filled with the Spirit, and to see my congregation moved and melted under the Word, as in great revival times, "the place shaken

where they are assembled together," because the Lord
has come in power.'

'The Lord puts a seal upon his own, that everybody
may know them. The sealing in your case is the Spirit
producing in you likeness to the Lord. The holier you
become, the seal is the more distinct and plain, the
more evident to every passer-by, for then will men
take knowledge of you that you have been with Jesus.'

SIN

'Right views of sin have a tendency to lead us to right
views of the person of the Saviour. But the converse
also is true: right views of the Saviour's person lead to
right views of sin.'

'Sin is not simply going against our conscience; it is
going against the law, though conscience keep silence.'

'Never trifle with one sin. It is like a little cloud
which, as a poet has said, may hold a hurricane
in its grasp. The next sin you commit may have
a mighty effect in the blighting of your life. You
do not know the streams that may flow from that
fountain; for sin is a fountain – not a mere act, but
a fountain of evil.'

'If ever there was anything that, more terribly than hell itself, showed the sinfulness of sin, it was the Saviour's agony in the garden.'

TROUBLES

'Into the furrows made by the plough of affliction and temptation, God casts the seeds of after-joy.'

'It sometimes seems hard to find out any reason for God's dealings with his children.'

'Now the Lord often sends sore afflictions upon his children in order that they may come and talk with him more.'

'The Master bore the Cross of atonement that he might make us righteous. He leaves us a cross of our own that we may be made holy.'

'Burdens are part of a believer's education.'

'A believer is an Aeolian harp, and every event of his life is just the passing wind drawing out the music. And God hears it.'

'God knows best how to ripen a soul for his own presence in glory.'

'We have got more from Paul's prison house than from his visit to the third heavens.'

'The Lord chooses our lot for us here, and he chooses our mansion for us above.'

'Never be offended at Christ's providences. He will recompense all to you, even in this life. "A hundredfold more in this life." O believer, keep him to his promise!'

'When God has wiped away every tear from our eyes we shall see his providences very clearly.'

'God's testimonies smooth the journey.'

'Those who sing loudest in the kingdom will be those who on earth had the greatest bodily suffering. We pity them now, but then we shall almost envy them.'

WITNESSING

'This, this incontrollable delight and testifying for the Lord, is the true spirit in which to engage in it – the

true missionary spirit in our bosom. Ourselves in the
suburbs of heaven, we tell of heaven.'

'The power to testify lies in our personal union to
the Lord, and in our so using the communion with
him that we abide in his presence, and are there filled
with his Spirit.'

WORSHIP

'How much more ought we to be joyous in our
heavenly Father's presence! We need not be always
singing. The heart has a silent language. There
is too little of adoration – simple worship – at
the present time.'

'A congregation of true worshippers is just
a congregation of those who think upon the Lord.'

GETTING OLD

'Yesterday and today I have had some glimpses within
the veil, as if to prepare me more for what may now
soon come. It is very solemn to find myself near the
threshold of eternity, my ministry nearly done, and

my long life coming to its close. Never was Christ to me more precious than he is now.'

'The night cometh, but thereafter the morning, the resurrection-morning, when we shall know the results of present labour, and when we shall see him as he is. It is a solemn thing to look back on so many years as I have had, and to look a little onward and see the eternal shore.'

'The Lord is kinder to me than ever, the nearer I come to the end of my journey.'

'It is a remark of old and experienced men that very few men, and very few ministers, keep up to the end the edge that was on their spirit at the first.'

'See that your last days are your best days.'

'I have been thinking tonight that perhaps my next great undertaking may be this: appearing at the judgment-seat of Christ, when I give an account of my trading with my talents.'

A LETTER TO HIS PARISHIONERS

Mount Carmel, June 29, 1839.

My Dear People, Beloved and Longed for,

The last time I wrote you we were at Alexandria in Egypt. Since then we have been in many various and new scenes, but the Lord has carried us safely through all. During the last two months we have been dwelling in tents, and travelling on asses and camels from place to place. The heat in this part of the world is very great at mid-day, so we set out on our journey early in the morning – sometimes before sunrise – and rest several hours when the day gets hot, under the shade of a tree – either olive, or palm, or fig. In the afternoon we travel on again some hours, and then pitch our tents and sleep for the night. We never travel on Sabbath; but on that day we rest; and though we have no public ordinances, yet we find it a happy season, while we read and meditate, and pray; – it is a time when we especially remember the Church at home, and our Parishes, and ask the outpouring of the Spirit to accompany the preaching of the Word throughout the day.

You will remember that living in tents was the manner in which the Patriarchs lived. I have often thought of Abraham pitching his tent under the oak of Mamre, and of Deborah under the palm-tree, and of many others – and I feel that God is explaining to me many things mentioned in Scripture, that I may explain them to you when I return. I trust that through your prayers he may so fill my soul, that when I see you again you may rejoice the more. I do not feel that distance, and new scenes, have made me forget you; on the contrary, the countries where we are shown to our very eyes the fulfilment of what God spoke, and the places where we have lately been, are places wherein most of the mighty works of Jesus were done; and when we are thus feeling the truth and reality of the things set before us in the Scriptures by the Holy Ghost, then we desire more than ever to come and bear witness of them to sinners.

There are few people who believe that God is sincere, and really intends to do every thing he says. Thoughtless, unconverted men will not be persuaded that he will do all he threatens, and will take their soul out of their body, and plunge it into hell. And many indolent and self-sufficient Christians will not believe that they might receive a hundredfold more joy and holiness than they have yet attained to, if they would only make better use of a full Saviour. Now I wish I could take such, and lead them to the village Emmaus, which lies on the side of a hill we saw near Jerusalem – for it was on the road to that village that Christ reproved two of his disciples, saying, 'O fools, and slow of heart to believe all that the prophets have spoken.'

In our journey through the Desert that lies between Egypt and the Holy Land, we were often fatigued and exhausted by the heat and the burning sand; yet the Lord preserved us, and brought us to the end. Part of that Desert is the Wilderness of Shur, where Hagar, Sarah's maidservant, had a vision from God, and was sent back to her mistress by God himself – teaching us that in the lowest station of life we may be near to God. Let servants among you remember this, and read over all about Hagar in Genesis 16 and 21; you will thus see that God requires you to submit yourselves to your masters, and at the same time he himself takes as much concern in your souls as in the souls of your masters.

The people who drive our camels and asses are descendants of Hagar's son, Ishmael. They are ignorant and unhappy. But there is a prophecy, that when the Jews are converted, and settled again in the Holy Land, these sons of Ishmael also shall be saved.

Isaiah foretells it in chapter 66:6, 7; and this should be another reason why you ought to pray much for the conversion of the Jews – there will be so many other nations converted after they have been brought in.

It was on June 1st that we entered the land of Israel. We crossed the channel of 'the River of Egypt', and found ourselves in the Plains that used to belong to the tribe of Simeon. It is a region for flocks and herds. We then went northward to Gaza; and in the olive groves and gardens near that city first heard the turtle dove, and the voice of other birds uniting with it – forming the very scene spoken of in the Song of Solomon, chapter 2:12: 'The flowers appear on the earth; the time of singing of birds is come, and the voice of the turtle is heard in our land' – in which words God tells the joy that Christ's coming will give to his people.

From Gaza we travelled to Jerusalem, through the valley of Eschol and the plain of Zephathah, famous for King Asa's victory. And here I wish to put you in mind how remarkable it was that God should cause our way to lie through Gaza, so that we came to Jerusalem by the very road which the Ethiopian Eunuch traversed, when 'he went on his way rejoicing'; – for you remember that was the last text I preached upon to you: the place, therefore, brought you all to my mind, and made me pray that you might in truth have that same joy in you for ever. One night on this road we heard the howling of a wolf; and, another morning, a wolf sprang across our path; which brought to my mind our Lord's parable, wherein he represents his people as safe in his fold from all such enemies. If any one, young or old, in all the parish of Collace, is not in Christ's fold, then that poor weak soul may become the prey of the wolf – of the Devil – this very night.

We were two Sabbaths in Jerusalem, and worshipped with the few Christians that are there, and I had also the privilege of preaching to them on Sabbath evening in an Upper Chamber on Mount Zion, where they met. There are indeed but few Christians here; for the Roman Catholics, who have a large Church here, are not Christians, except in name; and the rest of the people are mostly Jews or Mahometans. The Jews have here six synagogues, all of which we visited in turn; but the people are very poor and unhappy. If you saw them and their children growing up in ignorance, and the women not taught even to read: if you saw how little they care about their salvation, you would pity them, and long to send a missionary among them. No real Christian can live in Jerusalem without being deeply affected by all he sees. He walks the very streets over which Christ passed so often; he may climb Mount Zion, where the Tabernacle stood; he may go and look on Calvary, and remember that 'the blood of Christ cleanseth from all sin'; he may go out a little way from the town and see the Garden of Gethsemane, which is still marked by seven old olive trees; he may stand on the spot where Jesus wept over Jerusalem; and he may ascend the Mount of Olives from which Jesus went up to heaven, and where he foretold his second coming, and the end of the world, and bade us watch.

We were twice at Bethany, where Christ so often went in the evening, and where he comforted Martha and Mary when Lazarus died. Are any of you afflicted? Have any lost friends since I was among you? Go tonight to 'that same Jesus', and he will wipe away all tears from your eyes. Many of my young people will remember the Dead Sea, and how Jesus never visited it, because it is a type of hell, and no soul ever is redeemed if once in hell. Now, we see the Dead Sea from the Mount of Olives; and are thus, on the one hand, reminded of the way of salvation, when we look at the places where Jesus did his works of grace; and on the other hand, are reminded of the utter hopelessness of deliverance if we turn away from him. One day, we visited Bethlehem where the Angel told the glad tidings to the Shepherds, that there was a Saviour born for them. I am afraid that there are some among you so inattentive to your sinful state and wicked hearts that you never yet were really glad at the thoughts of a Saviour; if so, you are 'dead in sin', and are like the devils, who are troubled when they hear of Christ and wish he were away.

We have visited the Jews in almost every town of this country; they are all poor and none of them seem happy. The reason is, they have not the joy that Christ gives – his blood is upon them – they try to save themselves. Oh remember it is written, 'If any man love not the Lord Jesus, let him be Anathema Maranatha.' After leaving Jerusalem, the most interesting place we went to was Sychar, where Christ conversed with the woman at Jacob's Well. When looking at it, and sitting by it, I remembered that John 4, where the story is given, was the last chapter I read with my Sabbath Morning Class, and I asked for them all 'the living water, which springs up to everlasting life.' Ask the same for me in this dry and thirsty land.

A few days after, we arrived at Mount Carmel, and I did not forget my promise to pray for you there. We pitched our tent on the seashore, close under the hill, which is by the sea, as Jeremiah 46:18 mentions. It is so high, but once it was covered with vines and every fruitful tree to its very top, until the curse came on account of the sin of the land – 'the top of Carmel shall wither' (Amos 1:2). The brow that overhangs the sea, is the spot where Elijah prayed so perseveringly till the cloud appeared. Reminded by his example, and as next day was the Sabbath, I spent a season, just under that hill, in supplications for you – for the Parish in general, and for those that now minister to you; – in particular my Sabbath Morning Class came into my mind – then the assembled congregation – and after it the Sabbath School, where God's Spirit specially strives with you, my dear children, who are beginning your days: and, lastly, came the thought of you all on Sabbath Evenings, gathered in your families to talk over the word preached, and to help each other to apply it, as well as to teach it to your children, and unite in prayer. It would be glad tidings, indeed, to hear that the Holy Spirit is poured out on you, and that you are striving together for a full blessing, both in your closets and in prayer-meetings. We here see the palm tree flourishing in strength and beauty. May each believer among you inherit the promise of Psalm 92:12, 'The righteous shall flourish like the palm': even in this life may you have the victory over sin in the strength of Christ, which is signified in Revelation 7:9, by the glorious multitude who, because they had put on the white robes of the Redeemer's righteousness, were waving palms in their bands.

I hope that it is but a little season ere we shall see each other face to face, and recount the doings of the Lord. But, meanwhile, remember once more that God is dealing peculiarly with your Parish, even in this very act, that he is sending you the voice of entreaty and of exhortation from the mountains of Israel. Oh, my dear people, how often would Christ have gathered you! Are you willing to come to him that you may have life – are you all willing – and do you close with him for ever? He will soon appear in the clouds of heaven, and will name each of you. He will declare that all had a free salvation offered them, and if he needed a witness, he may summon even me to testify that it was so.

Commending you now to the Spirit of Truth and Grace,

I am, my dear People,

Yours in the Lord.

VISITATION OF THE SICK

Who are the sick? It is not a needless question by any means. We have known a wider opening of the hand follow upon the answer to the question, 'Who are the poor?' Certainly, 'the poor' are a larger class than many suppose, for they include institutions, as well as persons – all who must lean for help on the sympathy and help of others.

Who, then, are the sick? Perhaps it may open our hearts wider if we say, in reply to this question, they are all who, through any infirmity, are laid aside from active work, including frail and aged ones, and all who are under the cloud of sorrow. At the same time, those who live without God and without Christ in the world should know that they are not the persons who are spoken of as 'the sick' in the Word of God. It is God's sick ones to whom our attention is directed, and for whom our care is asked – members of Christ, in regard to whom he can say: 'In visiting them, even the least of them, you visited ME' (Matt. 25:36). The careless, godless, unconverted sick are undoubtedly to be sought out and visited; but he who is 'Saviour of all men, but specially of those who believe' (1 Tim. 4:10), in his peculiar love to his own, enjoins us, while doing good to all men, to care especially for those who are of the household of faith' (Gal. 6:10).

These sick ones, then, are so far commended to us for their comfort. We are to visit them. But a question meets us – for, it is written, 'Pure religion and undefiled before God and the Father is this, To visit the fatherless and widows in their affliction' (Jas. 1:27). Is not this statement extravagant? It seems to place the *visitation of the sick* in an extraordinary position. For surely this duty, however well performed, is not in itself even a certain evidence of the visitor's personal godliness. It is important, very important, on this account, to know the true meaning of that verse. The key to it is found in the word 'religion', a peculiar word in the original. It is *threskeia*, a term which speaks of the performance of Divine offices, or devout attention to the outward service of God; so much so, that Trench, in his *Synonyms of the New Testament*, explains it by *cultus exterior*, the external ceremonial or form by which the devout person is led to express his inward feeling. It is, in short, the attractive foliage and blossom on the tree, but in no sense whatever is it the root or the sap.

Our way is now clear to ask, How we are to proceed in carrying out this Visitation of the Sick?

It is well to notice that in Scripture 'visit' has, in one connection, attached to it as its object, *punishment*; and in another, *kindly help*. It is, of course, in this latter sense we use it when speaking of visiting the sick. There is ever in this use of it the suggestion of bringing help to the person in some form. In Genesis 50:24, 'God will surely visit you to bring you out of this land.' In Job 7:18, 'What is man that thou shouldst visit him every morning?' In Jeremiah 29:10, 'I will visit you and perform my good word toward you.' In Zephaniah 2:7, 'The Lord shall visit them and turn away their captivity.' In Luke 1:68, 'He hath visited and redeemed his people.' When the tears of the widow of Nain are wiped away, 'God hath visited his people' (Luke 7:16). How beautifully do the words of Psalm 65:9 express the effect of God's kind providence in springtime to the dry land:

Thou *visitest* the earth, and waterest it;
Thou dost greatly enrich it with the river of God.

And may we not suggest that even thus spiritually our visiting the sick might always 'water and enrich' till, as verse 13 says of the valleys and the pastures, we leave them so blessed, that

They shout for joy; they also sing.

A minister in Dublin, some years ago, made a call on one of his flock, a lady, who was feeble and rather desponding. When asked very tenderly about herself, her reply was, 'Weak – oh, so very weak!' And then she added that she had been that day much troubled in mind because she had found it impossible to govern her thoughts in meditation and prayer, so much so, that 'she had kept *going over the same things again and again*.' 'My dear friend,' replied her pastor, 'there is provision in the Gospel for you here. Our Lord Jesus Christ when his soul was exceedingly sorrowful, three times prayed, and spoke *the same words*.' In a moment her face lightened up. Her trouble was gone.

In similar circumstances, Dr. Stoughton, of London, entered the room of one sinking under pulmonary disease. 'How are you feeling today?' 'Weak – oh, so very weak!' He looked at her pale sad face, and, with half a smile on his own face, repeated two lines of a hymn well known to her:

> When I am weak, then I am strong;
> Grace is my shield, and Christ my song.

The effect was remarkable. Her countenance changed, lighted up with a gladness that never left it, but shone from it even in death.

'I am useless now – quite laid aside,' said a devoted Christian man in a time of sickness to a friend who came hoping to speak a word in season. The sick man was calm and patient. The words of his friend, however, seemed to aid him in no way, till, in going away, he said, with true feeling, 'You think you lie there useless; but the sight of you today has taught me what will send me on my way with stronger faith and confidence.' The idea of having helped another at once touched a chord in the heart of the sick believer, who was left in his chamber with his cup brimming over.

And it is true that the sick do help the whole in a multitude of ways. Let us tell them at times what their patient faith and joyous submission teach to those who come to help, but who go away helped by them. One reason for the long-continued and sore affliction of God's own may be specially to preach to us the lesson of Divine sovereignty, and to draw forth our sympathy more and more, that our own souls may become more like the heart of our Great High Priest.

Again, might we not sometimes suggest to God's suffering ones, who lament their utter inability to be of use for God's cause, that possibly they in a very special manner are giving one illustration of that text, 'To the intent that now *unto principalities and powers* might be known by the church the *manifold (polupoikilos) wisdom of God*' (Eph. 3:10). Angels who minister for the heirs of salvation may often be sent to the sick not to help, but to learn from them what they themselves can never know experimentally – viz., how the redeemed can pass through the hottest furnace, leaning on the Beloved. The same Holy Spirit who upheld the humanity of Christ on the cross, soul and body (Heb. 9:14), is upholding that suffering member of Christ's body; and angels 'look into these things' with intense interest. He is a teacher of *angels*!

In connection with this, it may be useful to remind the sick and feeble saint that *suffering* borne in Christ's name is real *service*. They think their soul is left empty, and they blame themselves for their unprofitableness. But falling in with the will of God is service, whether in the form of active doing, or passive submission and waiting. One day a pastor came to the bedside of a sick saint, and found her dull, low, sad. She did not use to be so; why was she so today? 'Oh, I have not been able since I awoke this morning till now to pray one petition, or offer praise, or even think over one verse.' The pastor had heard from the doctor that her trouble had taken a new turn, which had shaken her whole frame, and so he said, 'The Lord did not wish you today to pray, or praise, or remember any passage of Scripture.' 'What did you say?' 'The Lord today has taken from you the power to pray, or praise, or think to any purpose; he wishes you just to lie still and look up to him.' At once the cloud passed away. 'Oh, then, he is not angry! I can look to him as before.'

It is, at the same time, oftentimes seasonable to remind God's sick ones, that they must not give way to *selfishness*. The Lord expects them still to care for their fellowmen, and for the interests of his kingdom on the earth. It would be well for them to forget themselves in their remembrance of their Lord and his people, and of his afflicted in other places. Was not this the example left to us by our suffering Master?

If we were asked for some hints as to what is requisite by way of preparation for visiting the sick, we might suggest,

1. *The state of mind in which Christ was whenever he effected a cure*. It was this: 'Moved with compassion' (Mark 2:41). Very often are we told of him going forth to help, 'full of compassion.' With us there is a constant temptation to neglect this preparation. We are often compelled to go hurriedly to the sickbed; we are obliged to turn aside all at once from some other engrossing duty; we have scarcely had time to collect our thoughts for this more trying work. Yet we must be calm, and we must be patient, and we must be compassionate and kind, if we are to be really of use. Perhaps we might more readily find ourselves in the true frame for such visits, even when pressed beforehand by other business, if we on all occasions regarded visits to the sick as *opportunities of preaching and applying the Gospel*. We do not go to gossip, nor to speak of generalities; we do not go to relieve our consciences by repeating a text that seems appropriate, and to offer up a prayer. We go to carry the living water

of the Gospel to these hungry ones who cannot come to the public ordinances. Let us aim on all occasions to give them a fresh thought about him who 'once suffered for sins, the just for the unjust, to bring us unto God.' Should we not aim never to leave the room without pointing the sick one to the Lamb of God? Sometimes we will tell of his death, sometimes of his resurrection, sometimes of his intercession, sometimes of his coming again, and how he will then give the resurrection body, and wipe away all tears for ever.

2. Generally, *we should be brief*. It vexes a weak believer to find himself unable to follow the long prayer, or the many verses you read. Literally 'a word' spoken in due season may be our best way to be helpful; and that word, being a crumb of the Bread of life or a drop of the Water of life, has wondrous virtue in it, because it is the Word of God, which the Holy Spirit delights to use. A few fervent petitions and some short passage, like a live coal from the altar, will fill the soul of the infirm and sick and suffering with gladness.

There was once a godly elder, very dangerously ill, his face so swollen under erysipelas (a bright red rash) that he could neither see nor speak, nor could it be known whether or not he had the power to hear. The pastor used to come during the fortnight of his illness almost every day, doing no more than stand by him repeating a verse and praying over it. When that good man recovered, he most warmly thanked the pastor, telling him he heard every word each day, and how it helped him as if a voice from heaven spoke, when he could not call up a thought otherwise, adding that the very brevity of the interview was wonderfully in accordance with his feelings.

On another occasion the same pastor was asked to visit a bereaved widow, who was like Anna, the daughter of Phanuel, in that 'she trusted in God'. Before leaving he asked, 'Do you ever ponder that name of God – the Judge of the widow?' He explained that it spoke of God as managing the widow's affairs, attending to her interests, just as Samuel, Gideon, and the Judges of Israel did in behalf of the nation. After prayer, with a face of astonishment and relief, she said, 'You do not know how that one word has lifted off all my burdens!'

Nor was it with less joy that an intelligent but somewhat desponding saint caught at the words of Isaiah 27:3: 'Do you know,' he was asked, 'where this is? The Lord says of His vine, and every branch in it of course, "I will water it *every moment.*"' That *every moment* was enough to feast that now happy man for many days to come.

3. *In visiting unsaved persons*, there are errors we are apt to fall into. Partly from the desire to deal tenderly with them as sick ones, we are prone to be superficial in our conversation. It may be we see they are weak, not able to listen as they did in health, and so we excuse

ourselves for not trying to probe their conscience far; and so we are somewhat too easily satisfied. Oh how we need at such times to be 'full of the Holy Ghost', and to have him bringing very near to us that eternal world into which the dying one is so soon to enter! Let that warning of Ezekiel 13:22, ring in our ears: 'Ye have strengthened the hands of the wicked, that he should not return from his evil way, by *promising him life*.' At such a moment, a vague hope, an indefinite expression of assent to the Gospel cannot surely satisfy us. Can a man lean his weight upon a cloud? Or upon a shadow? No, he must see his bare foot resting on the Rock of Ages.

The writer will never forget the account one gave of his interview with an unsaved but anxious soul, to whom the doctor had told that death was close at hand – probably would be there in two hours. 'Oh,' said he, 'how I sought to make the way of salvation plainer and plainer. In a few moments that soul's eternity would be settled. With what trembling I sat by and spoke!' Was not this Paul's state of mind on ordinary occasions when pressing home the Gospel? 'I was with you in weakness, and in fear, and in much trembling' (1 Cor. 2:3). At such times how unspeakably precious is it to 'speak to the Breath' (Ezek. 37:9), for he gives life to the dry bones, and can at once take the things of Christ and show them.

We had to do with another case. The medical attendant thought it right to assure his patient that in a few weeks, as far as man could see, time would to her be for ever gone. This aroused her from spiritual torpor, and that very afternoon began an intensely earnest inquiry, 'What then must I do to be saved?' The Holy Spirit was there, and salvation came to that soul.

4. We should not forget to pray *for the body as well as the soul*. Occasionally, if much concerned about the soul of the sick one, we may omit to show sufficient sympathy for the state of the body. Christ never overlooked this matter. He cared for the seven disciples' cold and hunger that morning at the Sea of Tiberias, before he said a word to their conscience. He fed the 5000 almost as soon as he had taught them the things of the kingdom. 'You might next time try not to forget to ask the Lord for my bodily relief,' was the gentle rebuke given one day to the writer when bidding goodbye to a distressed man.

5. Do we pray for the sick in full *expectation of an answer*? Do we pray for them at home? Do we pray in the congregation for them, not as a mere duty, or because it will gratify the invalid, but because we surely look for an answer? Few pastors who have so prayed and watched but can tell of remarkable answers. As the servants of the Lord, are we never afraid that our *omissions* may yet trouble us sore – at least, may cause us sad regrets? We may look back and feel as

Livingstone did in the case of one over whom he thus laments: 'Poor Sebituane, my heart bleeds for thee. What would I not do for thee now? I will weep for thee till the day of my death. Alas! Alas! Sebituane! I might have said more to him. God forgive me! God free me from blood guiltiness! I might have recommended Jesus and his great Atonement more.'

But here we stop, though our subject might lead us on to many not unimportant points which we have not touched upon. We should like to have inquired into that most memorable passage in Job 33:23, where Elihu brings before us 'the Messenger, the Interpreter,' in the chamber of one chastened in his bed with pain, drawing near to the grave. We should like to have referred to the mystery of pain in the case of so many of God's people. Nor less should we have found it profitable to take up the case of Gaius, the friend of the beloved disciple, and of Epaphroditus, and Timothy, and Trophimus, not one of whom in their sickness got relief by miracle, though so dear to two of the greatest apostles. There must be some great blessing in sickness; (1) To the sick believer when his field lies fallow; (2) To those who wait on him (the Lord) and inhale the fragrance of the bruised spices; (3) To angels, of whom we spoke as here learning something of the manifold wisdom of God; and (4) beyond question, the day of Christ will show an immense revenue of glory to God.

THE LOVE OF THE FATHER

'For I came down from heaven, not to do mine own will, but the will of him that sent me. And this is the Father's will which hath sent me, that of all which he hath given me I should lose nothing, but should raise it up again at the last day. And this is the will of him that sent me, that every one which seeth the Son, and believeth on him, may have everlasting life: and I will raise him up at the last day' (John 6:38-40).

None of the evangelists or apostles speak so much of the Father as John, who knew most of his Son Jesus Christ, and leant upon his bosom. The reason is, John felt that the mind of *the Father* and the mind of *the Son* were the same – entirely the same. He was, therefore, engaged in the same topic when he unfolded the Father's love.

It is remarkable that it is this apostle who records what Jesus revealed concerning the Father, and how Jesus delighted to point his disciples to him. Thus, he shows us in the context, verse 37, that Jesus went into the secret of his pavilion when his soul was grieved by the perverse unbelief of men. In that hour, when Jesus could find no refreshment in the men around him, he turned back for a moment's joy to the Father's love. 'All that the Father giveth me shall come to me!' He bathes his soul in that depth of eternal love. He surveys those given to him – Abel, and the saints of his age – Abraham, and his faithful ones – Peter, John, Mary, Lydia – the few in Sardis – the souls under the altar – and, as he surveys them, he sees his Father's love sparkle from each one, for these are his Father's gift; and forthwith his own love overflows on all that stand by. He flashes out his own love when he in the same moment cries, 'And him that cometh to me, I will in no wise cast out.' It seems that in that hour he thought upon the future. He saw, as he uttered the words, 'All whom the Father giveth me,' how man would be prone to take this reference to the Father's love as indicating a difference between the grace of the Father and of the Son. He saw that many would say that Jesus damped the rising hope of the coming sinner when he said, 'All that the Father giveth me,' and therefore does he forthwith cast out that other cord of love, 'And him that cometh to me, I will in no wise cast out.' 'So great is my Father's love to me and to perishing men, that assuredly there shall be souls that come to me; and so great is my love and his love alike, that no coming one shall on any account be cast out.'

Dear brethren, if the snow had never lain on the tops of Lebanon, Jordan would never have been full or overflowing. There would have been no Saviour's grace for man to know and feel, if the Father had not 'so loved the world' as to give us his only begotten. Yet often is the Father's love suspected or forgotten, although he is the fountainhead, and all the streams of grace have had their source in him. 'Every good gift and every perfect gift is from above, and cometh down from the Father of lights' (Jas. 1:17). O brethren, we should love him as Jesus did. Come and see what wondrous reason there is why we should do so.

1. The Father's amazing love appears in his sparing this guilty world, though he spared not the angels that sinned. You know that it is the Father's part to arrange, and purpose, and decree – it is his to decide and appoint whatsoever cometh to pass. Now, in a past eternity, he had the case of this fallen world under consideration. He might have decreed immediate woe as soon as sin should be committed by men. For sin deserves not only *eternal*, but *immediate* curse; and he had seen meet so to determine in regard to those angels who should leave 'their first habitation'. But the barren fig-tree was spared – this most guilty world received a day of grace. It became the very theatre for

the display of long-suffering; so that our text exhibits to us the Son of God walking on a spared world, digging at the roots of its barren trees. 'Herein is love!' For to spare this whole world for a time, implied the intention of enduring man's rebellion and man's unceasing provocations, for at least six thousand years. It was equivalent to the Father saying, 'Lo! I will submit to bear man's apostacy – to allow him to provoke the eyes of my glory – to wag his head at me and say, "Can he see through the dark cloud?" – to cast up mire and the very filth of hell upon my pure white throne – nay, to aim at erasing my love from my own heart, and even strike at my own being!' O did it not require love ineffable ere this could be resolved upon! This guilty world's day of grace is a most marvellous proof and manifestation of Jehovah's depth of love. And, thou wicked and slothful servant, who sayest, 'He is an austere master,' shalt be confounded for ever. The Father needs do no more than point to this time of most undeserved longsuffering. You speak of mercy; and some of you say, 'He could not be a God of mercy if he cast away so many souls'; but already has his treatment of you displayed his mercy. Your day of grace proves him to be a loving God. O man, see to it before you are summoned to the Judgment Seat; for your plea, drawn from his mercy, is already dismissed. 'What will you do in the day of visitation?' You abuse your day – you sit down to eat and drink and rise up to play – you dance before your golden calf – and then complain of a long-suffering God, because his mercy bears with you only for a lifetime, and will not wink at your sin to all eternity.

2. The Father's amazing love appears in choosing some of this guilty world, who should certainly be to the praise of his glory. Our text refers to this in the expression, 'All that the Father hath given me.' And so at other times: 'Thou gavest them me' (John 17:6); and 'The men whom thou hast given me'; 'Blessed be the God and Father of our Lord Jesus Christ, according as he hath chosen us in him before the foundation of the world, having predestinated us to the adoption of children by Jesus Christ unto himself, according to the good pleasure of his will, to the praise of the glory of his grace, wherein he hath made us accepted in the beloved' (Eph. 1:5, 6).

Now, there was a mystery of love in this election. It lies in the fact that, but for this further determination of the Father, none of our world would after all have been saved. To give men full liberty to come and be saved is love indeed. To procure and provide a ransom available for all who do come, whatever they be, is love yet higher still. But love can ascend to a height beyond this – far beyond it. It has ascended infinitely higher, for it has resolved to draw many, many thousands to itself, who otherwise would not have come at all. The

Lord saw, dear brethren, that none in all this world would have – not one shipwrecked man would ever have swam to shore, for he hated the shore more than the very waves that lashed him. No manslayer would have crossed the threshold of the city of refuge; he would rather linger in the open plain and risk the blow of the avenger. No debtor would have deigned to accept the payment – no captive to receive the ransom; even though all was free – even though entreated to do so by God himself – even though hell was behind, and heaven before.

The world's corruption was deep beyond conception. Earth was an open sepulchre; and each man hated his God. It was in reference to what he saw of this fearful enmity that Jesus said, in melancholy pity, 'No man *can* come to me, except the Father which hath sent me draw him' (John 6:44). They are so totally depraved, they are so wedded to their lusts, they are so gross, and sensual – so truly dead in sin – they do not wish to be freed from their covetousness, their envy, their lust, their power to draw draughts of pleasure from ungodly revelry, or from intense engrossment with the lawful occupations of life. They hide among the trees of the garden at the first sound of the voice of the Lord, even when he comes with grace on his lips, and goodwill to men in his heart.

O brethren, to be able to love any of such a race, argues strange and mysterious depth of love in

God the Father. And he did fix his love on many of these; he did it freely, and he did it determinedly. So deliberate, decided, determined was this eternal love of the Father, that it made success certain in the case of each on whom it was fixed. It was such a love, that its plans and purposes implied the operation of each person of the Godhead. The *Spirit* must go forth and draw, and the Son go forth and die. This was the Father's plan! O what amazing love is here! What thoughts are in his heart to usward! He will not let go his purpose of having some of our fallen race standing round his throne.

(a) Anxious souls! Surely the God that would do this from all eternity, is a God of infinite grace. What a bosom is this to lean upon! What an inducement to draw near! Does it not confirm you in the belief of that declaration, 'Him that cometh unto me I will in no wise cast out!' He who makes such provision to ensure that many shall come, is one who will in nowise reject any that are coming!

(b) Unawakened men! There is nothing in the character of God that can account for your treatment of him; there is nothing in him or his ways that can excuse your hatred. It is the fearful depravity of your own souls that alone can account for your utter ungodliness. Your blood is on your own heads! Your heart may be as *deceitful* as it is *wicked*, so that you may not believe your own deplorable state of enmity; but Jehovah has said by the lips of his Son concerning all that thus resist him, 'Ye have hated me without a cause!'

3. The Father's amazing love appears in his giving Christ to be the sinner's way of salvation. It was he who made a new and living way for a sinner's return to him. '*This is the will of him that sent me*, that every one who seeth the Son and believeth on him may have everlasting life' (v. 40). '*God* so loved the world that he gave his only begotten Son, that whosoever believeth on him should not perish' (John 3:16). And hence the name given him in 2 Corinthians 1:3: '*The Father* of mercies'; and in Romans 8:32, 'He that spared not his Son.'

Had he for once caused one ray of the inaccessible light to shoot down to this earth in order to teach us our state of darkness – had he shown us one crown worn above, or one triumphal palm – had he caused us to hear one note of heavenly melody – all this would have left us inexcusable, if we did not ever after covet earnestly the things above. But he took the best gift in all his treasures; nay, he took the Son that was in his bosom, and gave him to man. Angels saw it done, and rapturously sang, 'To you is born a Saviour, who is Christ the Lord!' and all men that have had anointed eyes have responded as they gazed, 'To us a child is born! unto us a son is given!' It is by this measuring-line that you must fathom the depth of the ocean. It is by this fact that you must try to measure the unsearchable love of the Father. You test your fellow creatures' love by the sacrifices they would make for you. You judge of Abraham's love to his God by his sacrifice of Isaac. Now judge of the love of the Father by his gift of his Son.

It was the Father saying, 'I cannot give up my law and my holiness; for that would be ceasing to be God. I cannot hide my righteousness and resign its demands; for that would ruin all. I cannot put the burden on my angels; for they could not bear it one hour. I cannot leave it on man; for then, not one of them should ever stand before me. But this is my will. Awake, O sword, against my shepherd; let man be dipt in the blood of the Almighty's fellow!' He not only gave him, but substituted him in the room of the guilty – 'the just for the unjust, to bring us unto God.'

O brethren, the Father resolved that all salvation shall be found in the Son. He carefully avoided leaving any of the details of salvation for us to perform. The Father was he who provided that the chastisement of our peace should be laid upon another; and no atoning tears left for us to shed – no atoning suffering left for us to endure – not one atoning sigh left for us to heave. Therefore, 'it pleased *the Lord* to bruise *him*; he put *him* to grief' (Isa. 53:10); and this he did with such calm, decided love, that the appeal of his beloved Son to him, 'Father, if it be possible, let this cup pass,' served only to manifest his long-settled and unchanging plan.

He had resolved that he should have children and sons from among men; but he had further resolved that their way of becoming his children and sons should all express his love. It was to be free; they were to come to him from the far country 'in a chariot paved with love'. All he asked of them was, that they should ascend the chariot and be carried home; for as many as received Jesus were at once to receive the privilege of sons of God. 'Behold, what manner of love *the Father* hath bestowed on us, that we should be called sons of God' (1 John 3:1); but equally amazing that we should become sons in a way so free. It costs Jesus all; it costs us nothing. Every drop of the vial falls on Jesus, and not even the dregs are left. Every arrow that was needed to express the Lord's hatred of sin and vindicate his law, sinks into the heart of Jesus, and is aimed at him by the Father's hand! All penalties are exacted of him; all obedience is rendered by him; and all this is done according to, and in exact fulfilment of, the Father's purpose of love to us. These are just the thoughts of the Father toward us, carried out into accomplishment.

Now, brethren, the Father, having given us this way and warrant for coming to him, manifests his love yet more by shutting you up to the necessity of taking this one way, this only warrant. 'Everyone that hath heard and learnt of the Father cometh unto me' (John 6:45), said Jesus; and 'no man cometh unto the Father but by me' (John 14:6). You are reduced to the necessity of being saved by a free salvation. It is written, 'Him hath God the Father sealed' (John 6:27). He has made Jesus to be your Joseph; he has given him the royal signet. When you cry for bread, he says to all, 'Go to Joseph' (Gen. 41:55). Jesus has the seal of the Father. O with such a warrant, and going to one whose love is such that it planned this way, one whose bosom is filled with calm, determined, eternal love, can you hesitate as to duty? Can you hesitate as to the way of safety? Nothing but enmity on your part, and deep-rooted dislike, can account for your resting contented without possession of the Father's gift. What more will you venture to say the Father ought to have given? See what he has already given, and given without any claim on your part. If you are lost, your ruin will lie on yourself. Will ever your blasphemous lips dare to lay your damnation to the charge of such a God? Oh, fall in with his plan of grace! The plan that such a God proposes, must be one worthy of such a sinner's immediate acceptance. And *immediate acceptance* is the only manner in which such a sinner can show any due sense of the *free grace* of his God.

You who do already believe, be reminded that it is to the Father you owe all your peace, and joy, and blessed assurance of eternal life. You were once far off;

and once you were only anxiously wishing to find his favour. But he showed your anxious souls his economy of grace – he brought you to drink of his living waters that are without price – he spread out the warrant before your eyes, and you were made to see that there was nothing left for you to complete. The Father's plan was so gracious, that, in seeing the Son, you saw a finished salvation. Oh, give glory evermore at once to 'him that sitteth on the throne, and to the Lamb.'

4. The amazing love of the Father appears in his revealing himself to us – he does not act through an interpreter only, but he makes himself known. He gives us, as it were, the means of searching and trying his heart, that we may be quite sure of his whole mind towards us, and that his matchless character may draw our souls to himself.

He does this through the incarnation of Jesus. For we are told in our text, 'I came down from heaven not to do mine own will, but the will of him that sent me' – that is, not to exercise any separate will of mine as man, but as man to exhibit and to do the Father's will. All, therefore, that is in Christ, expresses the mind of his Father also. 'I am in the Father, and the Father in me' (John 14:10). 'He that hath seen me hath seen the Father' (John 14:9).

O brethren, there is manifold love in his revelation to us of the Father. It is not only that our suspicious hearts would never have been quite at rest unless we had thus known the Father also; but it gives us a view of his willingness to condescend to us in any way that may more fully draw us, or be more likely to induce us to love 'the Lord our God with all our heart, and all our soul, and all our mind, and all our strength.' He seems herein to come out of his 'light inaccessible', that he may become known to his fallen creatures. This is like humiliation; it is the Father's condescension. If Solomon, in order to engage the confidence of some loathsome leper, had come forth in all his glory, in his royal apparel, and with his golden sceptre, then would all the land have rung with the story of his condescending kindness. And it is not less that our God has done. He has come forth that we might know him. He has put on the robe of humanity, wherein he could be best looked upon by our mortal eye, and he has shown himself in all his grace and attractive love to a fallen world.

Herein is love! the Father will go to the utmost length in order to draw you back from the pit. Like the Grecian mother who, by her song, drew back her wilful child from the edge of the awful precipice, and brought it to her bosom secure; so the Lord, by the discovery of his infinitely glorious and gracious nature, would draw you from your sin. He would present to your idolatrous and adulterous eyes a sight more attractive than earth, in its softest forms, can furnish. He would keep you back from hell, O sinner, by manifesting himself to you as altogether lovely! O how deep is your corruption! How strong your enmity! How unconquerable your perversity! You hate *God*, after seeing him revealed in Jesus! Every exhibition of greatness, mingled with grace in Jesus, was the revelation of *the Father* also! Every discovery of patience, long-suffering, and grieved love – every time Jesus went apart to weep in secret places for the pride of men, it was the Father's feeling also. When Jesus beheld Jerusalem, and wept over it, O there was a tender pity there that just pictured forth the Father's yearning compassion – as if the Father himself had come forth from the 'light inaccessible', and had spoken in the hearing and sight of men, '*How* shall I give thee up, Ephraim; *how* shall I deliver thee, Israel? *How* shall I make thee as Admah, and set thee as Zeboim?'

Nor is it less the Father's mind, when Jesus cries in your ears, 'Him that cometh unto me I will in nowise cast out.' This is the Father's will who has sent him. As if he knew that you might say, on hearing that it is certain that all shall come who are given to Christ, 'Ah, then, perhaps though I were to come, I would not be welcomed,' the Saviour says, and the Father speaks by his lips, 'Him that cometh I will in no wise cast out.' You shall never be rejected, if you come – never on the ground that you were too great a sinner – never on the ground that, though you come, you were not given to Christ. 'You shall in nowise be cast out.' Any question regarding the Father's secret purposes, or the Father's accurate foreknowledge of who are his own – any question of this sort is quite out of your province. It is *friends* who get acquainted with the *secrets* of another's heart; it is not strangers. You are to come on the strength of the *warrant alone*; and so you will become a friend and a child of his family, and be no more cast out.

5. The Father's amazing love appears in appointing the eternal reward for redeemed sinners. Our text says, 'I came down to do the will of him that sent me,' and 'this is the Father's will that hath sent me, that of all which he hath given me I should lose nothing, but should raise it up again at the last day' (John 6:39). Therefore, says Jesus, 'I *will* raise him up at the last day' (v. 40).

It is remarkable how the Father delights to honour the Son while wearing our nature. It is of him in our nature, nay, in the act of bearing away, like the scapegoat, our sins on his person, that it is written, 'Therefore doth the Father love me, because I lay down my life, and take it up again' (John 10:17). It is in our nature that he is to judge, and to him every knee shall bow, and every tongue confess when he appears, clothed in our nature, and wearing the many crowns of this earth's dominion. Now, *love to him in our nature* is love *to us*. O, then, brethren, read here the *Father's* delight in our race. He takes our nature, in the person of Jesus, to his nearest presence; he sheds round it, in the person of Jesus, his brightest beams; he places it on his right hand in majesty.

But farther, it is written here, that the rising of the believers in the resurrection of the just is appointed of the Father – 'that I should raise it up again at the last day.' It is he who has purposed the glorious triumph over death, which believers gain in the resurrection morn.

It is he who planned that they should live and reign with Christ, blessed and holy, children of the first resurrection, and never subject to the second death. It is he who blesses them; for the King shall say, 'Come ye blessed of *my Father*' (Matt. 25:34). It is he who bestows the kingdom upon them: 'I appoint unto you a kingdom, as my Father hath appointed me' (Luke 22:29). It is he who gives them power over the nations; for Christ in giving his power says, 'Even as I received of my Father' (Rev. 2:27). It is the Father who introduces them to the glory of Christ (John 17:24). It is in *the Father's* house they dwell – in his many mansions (John 14:2). And even as Jesus went to the Father, so do they; for they are 'with him where he is,' in the immediate presence of the Father.

Thus, brethren, every token of love, in that blessed kingdom, bears the impress of the Father's grace. Every glory there sparkles with beams of the Father's love. O what a God of love is our God. And it is to his bosom the returning sinner comes. Sweet and blessed hope! to be near him, to try the depths of his heart – to have access through Jesus in our nature to his bosom – and so to be able to pour out our heart to him, and feel him pour out his to us. This is life eternal.

A child of God once asked, in meditating on the words – 'Where thou causest thy flock to rest' – where this resting-place might be thought to be? One said, 'In Jesus.' But the other replied, 'It is even in the Father's bosom.' And truly this is a believer's deepest rest. 'By him we believe in God' (1 Pet. 1:21), that is, the Father; and 'we come unto God by him' (Heb. 7:25). It is your place of rest, believer. It is the inner apartment of the pavilion – the secret of the tent. It is the farthest off spot from earth, it is out of sight of its pleasures, joys, gain, ambition. 'Love not the world, neither the things of the world; if any man love the world, *the love of the Father is not in him*' (1 John 2:15). 'Little children, *ye have known the Father*' (v. 13).

O beloved, before I conclude, let me once more cast out the cords of love to draw the rebellious among you. This God is our God. This is he who assures you of his desire for your salvation, 'I have no pleasure at all in the death of him that dieth, saith the Lord, but rather that he turn from his ways and live.' You are the worm that tried to crawl up to his throne, and to sit down as sovereign, and yet he has not crushed you! Your bosom is the seat of fearful sin, hatred of the holy one, dark suspicions of his sincerity, fond plans of self-exaltation, selfish schemes for present indulgence, ungodly fancies, sensual, earthly, devilish desires. Yet still our God, even *the Father*, laments over you. He takes no blame to himself for your wretched degradation; for, on the contrary, he has at every step cast hindrances in your way to hell. He laments over you, 'O Israel, thou hast destroyed thyself, but in me is thy help found!' He loved Jesus all the more for dying and rising again (John 10:17), because it opened up the channel of love; it gave vent to his love to man. Only draw near and see this ocean. It is the same ocean of love which is seen when you look on a dying Saviour; but it is the same ocean seen from another point of view. And what can exceed the power of the appeal which God hereby makes to you, when he declares, '*That* it is not the love of the Son alone, but the unbought, free, eternal love of Godhead!' It is *the Father* who lays down Jesus for a foundation-stone, and cries to a careless world, 'Behold! I lay in Zion for a foundation, a stone, a tried stone, a precious corner-stone.' It is *the Father* who calls and invites, 'Behold! my servant whom I have chosen! mine elect in whom *my soul* delighteth!' It is the Father who points to the cross and cries to all the earth, 'I, even I am he who blotteth out thy transgressions for mine own name's sake, and will not remember thy sins.' This is the Father's will, and Christ himself is the herald that proclaims it to a lost world, 'This is the will of him that sent me, that every one which seeth the Son and believeth on him may have everlasting life!'

Christian Focus Publications

Our mission statement —

STAYING FAITHFUL

In dependence upon God we seek to impact the world
through literature faithful to His infallible Word, the Bible.
Our aim is to ensure that the Lord Jesus Christ is presented as
the only hope to obtain forgiveness of sin, live a useful life and
look forward to heaven with Him.

Our books are published in four imprints:

CHRISTIAN
FOCUS

Popular works including biographies, commentaries, basic doctrine
and Christian living.

CHRISTIAN
HERITAGE

Books representing some of the
best material from the rich heritage
of the church.

MENTOR

Books written at a level suitable
for Bible College and seminary
students, pastors, and other serious
readers. The imprint includes
commentaries, doctrinal studies,
examination of current issues and
church history.

CF4•K

Children's books for quality Bible
teaching and for all age groups: Sunday
school curriculum, puzzle and activity
books; personal and family devotional
titles, biographies and inspirational sto-
ries — because you are never too young
to know Jesus!

Christian Focus Publications Ltd,
Geanies House, Fearn, Ross-shire,
IV20 1TW, Scotland, United Kingdom.
www.christianfocus.com
blog.christianfocus.com